Algorithmic Trading vs. S&P 500, FTSE 100, OMX Stockholm 30 Index

Tom Gardiner

Abstract

The research at hand aims to define effectiveness of algorithmic trading, comparing with different benchmarks represented by several types of indexes. How big returns can be gotten by algorithmic trading, taking into account the costs of informational and trading infrastructure needed for robot trading implementation?

To get the result, it's necessary to compare two opposite trading strategies:

1) Algorithmic trading (implemented by high-frequency trading robot (based on statistic arbitrage strategy) and trend-following trading robot (based on the indicator Exponential Moving Average with the Variable Factor of Smoothing))
2) Index investing strategy (classical index strategies "buy and hold", implemented by four different types of indexes: Capitalization weight index, Fundamental indexing, Equal-weighted indexing, Risk-based indexation/minimal variance).

According to the results, it was found that at the current phase of markets' development, it is theoretically possible for algorithmic trading (and especially high-frequency strategies) to exceed the returns of index strategy, but we should note two important factors:

1) Taking into account all of the costs of organization of high-frequency trading (brokerage and stock exchanges commissions, trade-related infrastructure maintenance, etc.), the difference in returns (with superiority of high-frequency strategy) will be much less (see more in section *4.3 Organization of trading infrastructure. Development of trading robots*).
2) Given the fact that "markets' efficiency" is growing every year (see more about it further in thesis), and the returns of high-frequency strategies tends to decrease with time (see more about it further in thesis), it is quite logical to assume that it will be necessary to invest more and more in trading infrastructure to "fix" the returns of high-frequency trading strategies on a higher level, than the results of index investing strategies.

Table of Contents

Appendices

Figures

Tables

1 Introduction

Substantial development of information technologies (IT) stimulated the beginning of "electronic revolution", which allowed market participants to use all the accessible market services without the need of physical presence in exchanges centers. For relatively short period of time, IT led to dramatically increased automation of order-execution process.

From the end of 1990s, the electronification of market orders' execution made it possible to transmit orders electronically, but not by telephone, mail, or in person, as it was before that, and, as a result, the biggest part of trading on modern world financial markets is implementing by internet and computer systems (Chlistalla, 2011). This fact, obviously, made it possible to use different trading algorithms widely in everyday trading practice.

Algorithmic trading (AT) is a broad term that can describe quite a wide range of methods and different techniques. It is crucial to understand that algorithmic trading should not be necessary associated with the speed of decision making and sending orders. These things characterize a subgroup of algorithmic trading, which is called high-frequency trading (HFT). Originally, AT was mainly used for managing orders, as an attempt to decrease market influence by optimizing trade execution.

"Hence, algorithmic trading may be defined as electronic trading whose parameters are determined by strict adherence to a predetermined set of rules aimed at delivering specific execution outcomes" (Chlistalla, 2011).

Robot trading usually can be defined by setting up following list of parameters (Hendershott, 2011):

1) Timing (or using time frame)
2) Price, quantity and routing of orders
3) Dynamically monitoring market conditions across different securities and trading venues
4) Reducing market impact by optimally breaking large orders into smaller ones
5) Tracking benchmarks over the execution interval

High-frequency trading (HFT) is a subset of algorithmic trading where a large number of orders (which are usually fairly small in size) are sent into the market at high speed, with round-trip execution times measured in microseconds (Brogaard, 2010).

The algorithmic trading is widely used both by institutional investors, for the efficient execution of large orders, and by proprietary traders and hedge funds for getting speculative profit. In 2009, the share of high-frequency algorithmic trading accounted for about 73% of the total volume of stocks trading in the U.S. According to Finansinspektionen report (February 2012), approximately 83% of market participants used algorithmic trading in 2011, and approximately 12% of market participants used high-frequency trading on Swedish market. On the MICEX in 2010, the share of high-frequency systems in the turnover of stock market was about 11-13%, while the number of orders evaluated as 45%. According to RTS (Russian Trading System), in 2010 the share of trading robots in the turnover of derivatives market on RTS FORTS section accounted for approximately 50% and their share in the total number of orders at certain times reached 90%

But, at the same time, the question of the efficiency of algorithmic trading systems has not been resolved completely. Taking into account, that there is a need in developing informational and trading infrastructure, special software and additional costs for brokerage and exchange commission, the final results of algorithmic trading implementation are not so clear. Especially, if we think about a lot of variable investing alternatives: like investing in different types of indexes – as the most famous benchmark.

Accordingly, here investors face a dilemma:

Do investors really need to develop the trading robots and create appropriate informational and trading infrastructure in a hope to "outperform the market", or it is enough just to get average market return, corresponding with the average market risk?

2 Purpose and research question

The purpose of this study is an attempt to check, if algorithmic trading can be more effective, than passive investing strategy. Namely, can algorithmic trading get the bigger returns, than index? What should investor do: to develop the trading robots and create appropriate informational and trading infrastructure in a hope to "outperform the market", or it is enough just to get average market return, corresponding with the average market risk?

To get the result, it's necessary to compare two opposite trading strategies:

1) **Algorithmic trading** (implemented by high-frequency trading robot (based on *statistic arbitrage strategy*) and trend-following trading robot (based on the indicator *Exponential Moving Average with the Variable Factor of Smoothing*))
2) **Index investing strategy** (classical index strategies *"buy and hold"*, implemented by four different types of indexes: *Capitalization weight index, Fundamental indexing, Equal-weighted indexing, Risk-based indexation/minimal variance*).

For this study analysis, there were chosen three stock market indexes:

1) **S&P 500** (the U.S. index of "broad market")
2) **FTSE 100** (the UK) - *since these two markets are ones of the biggest in capitalization and most liquid (and, for this reason, most "efficient" in terms of the Efficient Market Hypothesis)*
3) **OMX Stockholm 30 Index (Sweden)** - *in order to check whether the Swedish stock market acts as well as its larger global counterparts.*

To make the results more relevant, I considered the period of time from 01.01.2003 to 01.01.2012, when the previous crisis of 2001-2002 (the "DotCom bubble") has been overcome, but, nevertheless, I considered the period of crisis 2007-2009 too, because of increase in volatility (since it strongly effects the returns of index strategies).

There were examined several different investment horizons: from 1 year up till 10 years in the periods before and after the global financial crisis (2007-2009).

Using the trading robots, I tested historical quotes of three indexes (S& P500, FTSE100 and OMX Stockholm 30 Index) on the time interval from 01.01.2003 to 01.01.2012 in different "time dimensions": 5 minutes, 15 minutes, 1 hour, 4 hours, one day.

Thus, for each of the selected stock market indexes, we have the opportunity to see at what "market phase" (year) and in which "time dimension» (M5, M15, H1, H4, D1) robot trading strategy would show the most successful results, and then to compare these results with the results of the passive (index) trading strategies.

Research questions:

> Which investing strategies – algorithmic trading or investing in index – could bring bigger returns to investors for period from 01.01.2003 to 01.01.2012?

- Which investing strategies – algorithmic trading or investing in index – got bigger returns in the period of crisis 2008-2009?
- In which 'time dimension" (M5, M15, H1, H4, D1) can algorithmic trading strategies get biggest returns?
- For which "market phases" (trend or flat) can algorithmic trading strategies be used in the most optimal way?
- Does "market efficiency" have the same value when we move from small to larger "time dimension", and does it stable other considered period of time (2003 – 2012)?

3. Previous studies and theoretical framework

3.1 Conception of algorithmic trading. Literature, approaches and methods

Substantial development of information technologies (IT) stimulated the beginning of "electronic revolution", which allowed market participants to use all the accessible market services without the need of physical presence in exchanges centers. For relatively short period of time, IT led to dramatically increased automation of order-execution process.

From the end of 1990s, the electronification of market orders' execution made it possible to transmit orders electronically, but not by telephone, mail, or in person, as it was before that, and, as a result, the biggest part of trading on modern world financial markets is implement by internet and computer systems (Chlistalla, 2011).

This fact, obviously, made it possible to use different trading algorithms widely in everyday trading practice.

Algorithmic trading is a formalized process of making deals on the financial markets based on a given algorithm and using special computer systems (trading robots) (Lati, 2009).

Algorithmic trading (AT) is a broad term that can describe quite a wide range of methods and different techniques. It is crucial to understand that algorithmic trading should not be necessary associated with the speed of decision making and sending orders. These things characterize a subgroup of algorithmic trading, which is called high-frequency trading (HFT). Originally, AT was mainly used for managing orders, as an attempt to decrease market influence by optimizing trade execution.

"Algorithmic Trading may be defined as electronic trading whose parameters are determined by strict adherence to a predetermined set of rules aimed at delivering specific execution outcomes" (Chlistalla, 2011).

Robot trading usually can be defined by setting up following list of parameters (Hendershott, 2011):

1) Timing (or using time frame)

2) Price, quantity and routing of orders

3) Dynamically monitoring market conditions across different securities and trading venues

4) Reducing market impact by optimally breaking large orders into smaller ones

5) Tracking benchmarks over the execution interval

High-frequency trading (HFT) is a subset of algorithmic trading where a large number of orders (which are usually fairly small in size) are sent into the market at high speed, with round-trip execution times measured in microseconds (Brogaard, 2010).

Possible definitions of algorithmic and high-frequency trading that are mainly used in academic literature and papers can be found in Table and Table in Appendix 5.

"Programs running on high-speed computers analyze massive amounts of market data, using sophisticated algorithms to exploit trading opportunities that may open up for milliseconds or seconds. Participants are constantly taking advantage of very small price imbalances; by doing that at a high rate of recurrence, they are able to generate sizeable profits. Typically, a high frequency trader would not hold a position open for more than a few seconds. Empirical evidence reveals that the average U.S. stock is held for 22 seconds." Chlistalla (2009, p. 3).

As Chlistalla (2011) writes, *the first generation of algorithms* were quite simple in terms of goals and logic – they were just trade execution algorithms.

The second generation of algorithms already implemented some trading strategies and became much more sophisticated: they usually started to use for generating of trading signals, which were then executed by trade execution algorithms.

Third generation of algorithms started to implement intelligent logic that learns from market activity and adjusts the trading strategy of the order based on what the algorithm perceives is happening in the market.

The algorithmic trading is widely used both by institutional investors, for the efficient execution of large orders, and by proprietary traders and hedge funds for getting speculative profit.

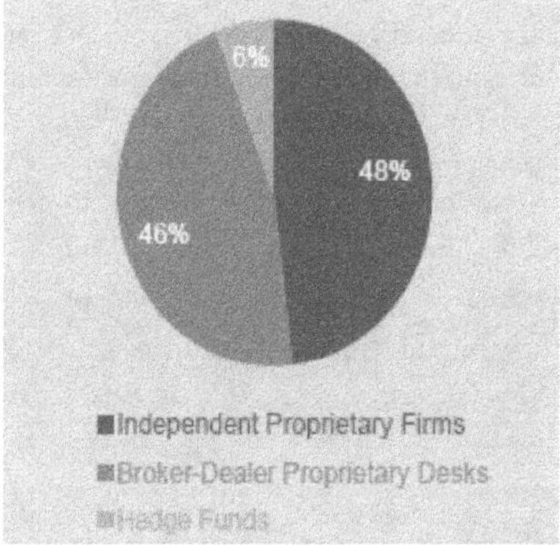

Figure 1. High-frequency trading volumes (U.S. equities)
Source: TABB Group, 2010

In 2009, the share of high-frequency algorithmic trading accounted for about 73% of the total volume of stocks trading in the U.S. (Lati, 2009).

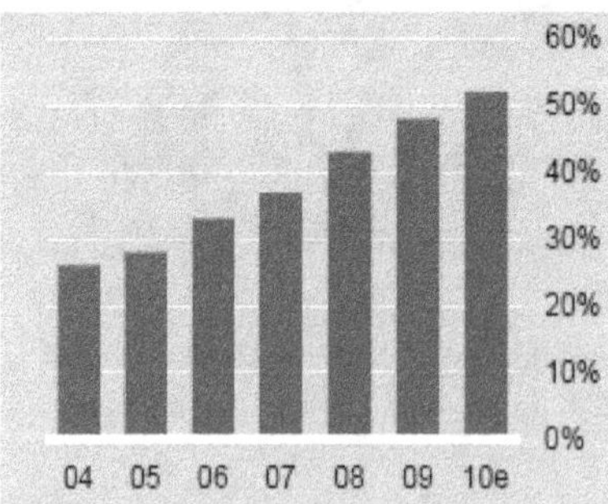

Figure 2. Adaptation of algorithmic execution (% of total U.S. equities trading volume)

Source: Aite Group, 2010

On the MICEX in 2010, the share of high-frequency systems in the turnover of stock market was about 11-13%, while the number of orders evaluated as 45%. According to RTS, in 2010 the share of trading robots in the turnover of derivatives market on RTS FORTS section accounted for approximately 50% and their share in the total number of orders at certain times reached 90% (Smorodskay 2010).

According to Finansinspektionen report *Investigation into high frequency and algorithmic trading* (February 2012), approximately 83% of market participants used algorithmic trading in 2011, and approximately 12% of market participants used high-frequency trading on Swedish market.

Detailed information about the share of algorithmic high-frequency trading on world stock exchanges can be found in Appendix 1.

As Aldridge (2009) writes "for a market to be suitable, it must be both liquid and electronic to facilitate the quick turnover of capital. Based on three key elements of each market:

1) Available liquidity
2) Electronic trading capability
3) Regulatory considerations

It is possible to systematize different assets with respect to the optimal frequency of its' usage for high-frequency trading." Let's illustrate it in Figure 3.

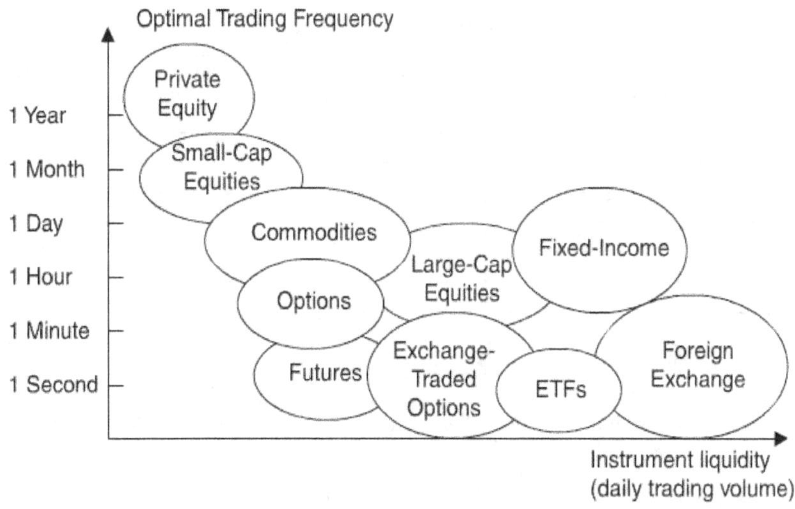

Figure 3. Optimal trading frequency for various trading instruments, depending on the instrument's liquidity.

Source: Aldridge, I., 2009, *High-Frequency Trading: A Practical Guide to Algorithmic Strategies and Trading Systems, John Wiley & Sons,* p.39

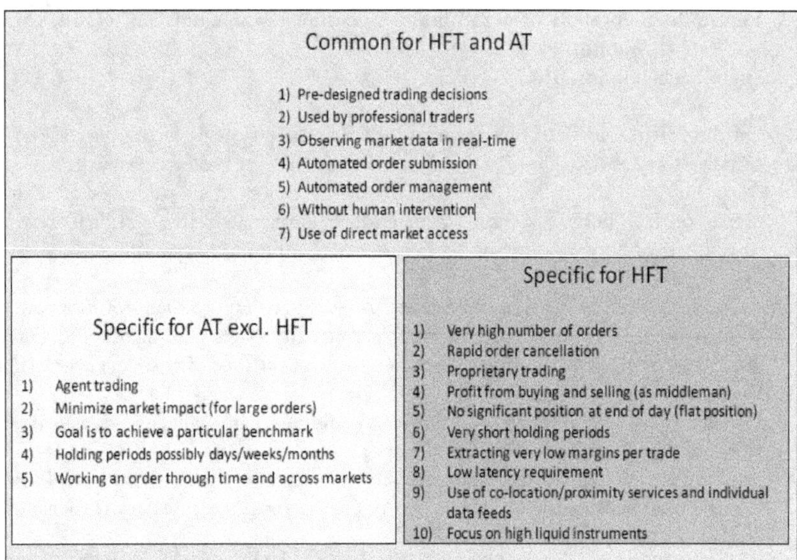

Figure 4. Overview of algorithmic and high-frequency trading
Source: Gomber, et. al., (2011). *High-Frequency Trading*

According to the TRADE Annual Algorithmic Survey, the main reasons for using algorithms in trading are:

Table 1. Reasons for using algorithms in trading

Reason for using algorithms	Popularity of reason among market participants' (% of all answers in survey)
Anonymity	22
Cost	20
Trader productivity	14
Reduced market impact	13
Speed	11
Ease of use	7
Execution consistency	6
Customization	4
Other	3

Source: Deutsche Bank, *High frequency trading – Better than its reputation*, Research note, February 2011

Among experts, academics and practitioners there a lot of discussion about the possible influence of high-frequency trading on markets, namely, on market efficiency. Some experts (Hendershott, Riordan, 2009; Jovanovic, Menkveld, 2010) note, that high-frequency trading can provide market with liquidity, decrease spreads and helps align prices across markets, if it is implemented as market-making or arbitrage strategy.

0.030
0.025
0.020
0.015
0.010
0.005
-
03 04 05 06 07 08 09
Median S&P 500 Bid-Ask Spread

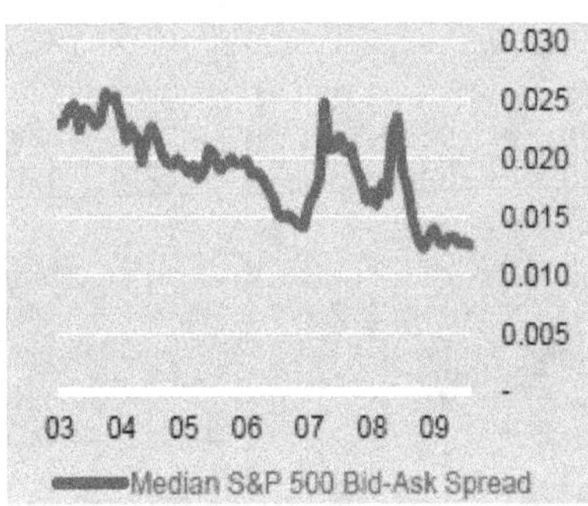

Figure 5. Bid-Ask Spread Reduction (USD)
Source: Deutsche Bank, *High frequency trading – Better than its reputation*, Research note, February 2011

But, according to Chlistalla (2011), though there is no exact evidence in academic literature, that high-frequency trading makes negative influence on market equality, still there some concerns:

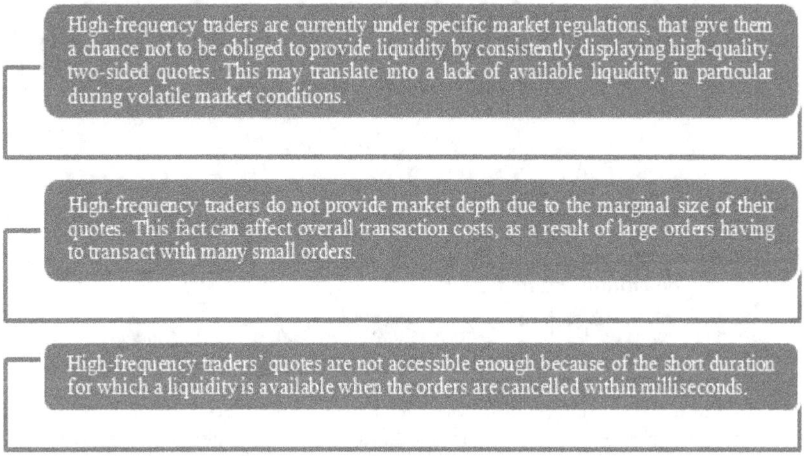

High-frequency traders are currently under specific market regulations, that give them a chance not to be obliged to provide liquidity by consistently displaying high-quality, two-sided quotes. This may translate into a lack of available liquidity, in particular during volatile market conditions.
High-frequency traders do not provide market depth due to the marginal size of their quotes. This fact can affect overall transaction costs, as a result of large orders having to transact with many small orders.
High-frequency traders' quotes are not accessible enough because of the short duration for which a liquidity is available when the orders are cancelled within milliseconds.

Figure 6. Possible negative impacts of high-frequency trading

Source: Deutsche Bank, *High frequency trading – Better than its reputation*, Research note, February 2011

Also, it is very interesting question to check if high-frequency trading contributes to the price formation process on equities markets. As Deutsche Bank (High frequency trading – Better than its reputation, Research note, February 2011) writes "in this context, Brogaard (2010) examines a large data set of HFT firms trading on NASDAQ and finds that:

High-frequency traders add substantially to the price formation process as they tend to follow a price reversal strategy (irrespective of whether they are supplying liquidity or demanding it), driven by order imbalances, and so tend to stabilise prices.

High-frequency traders do not seem to systematically front-run non-HFTs. They provide the best bid and offer quotes for a significant portion of the trading day, but only around a quarter of the book depth (as do non-HFTs) and reduce their supply of liquidity only moderately as volatility increases.

High-frequency traders engage in a less diverse variety of strategies than non-HFTs, which may exacerbate market move-ments if HFTs use similar trading strategies.

While in principle high cancellation rates could impact the smoothness of execution in markets where high-frequency traders are present, prevailing narrow spreads seem to suggest that cancelled quotes are quickly replaced by other market participants. Hendershott and Riordan (2009) find that algorithmic traders' quotes play a larger role in the price formation process than human quotes.

Figure 7. Contribution of high-frequency traders to the price formation process on equities markets.

Source: Deutsche Bank, *High frequency trading – Better than its reputation*, Research note, February 2011

As a result, from one point of view, high-frequency traders help to detect and correct anomalies in market prices. From another point of view, high-frequency traders might distort price formation if it creates an incentive for natural liquidity to shift into dark pools as a way of avoiding trans-acting with ever-decreasing order sizes

3.1.1 The main types of algorithmic strategies

Despite the variety of existing algorithmic strategies, most of them use the general principles of trading signal's construction or similar algorithms, which allow us to combine them in couple of groups.

From the perspective of the "main goal", strategies can be divided into two broad categories: *execution strategies and speculative strategies* (Katz, *2000)*.

> It is necessary to stress that, as Chlistalla (2011, p. 3) writes
>
> "HFT is not a strategy per se but rather a technologically more advanced method of implementing particular trading strategies. The objective of HFT strategies is to seek to benefit from market liquidity imbalances or other short-term pricing inefficiencies."

1) Execution strategies

These strategies solve the problem of buying or selling large orders of financial instruments with a minimum difference of the final weighted average transaction price from the current market price of the instrument. This category of strategies is actively used by investment funds and brokerage firms around the world.

According to *Katz (2000)*, there are three most common algorithms among execution strategies

1.1) *Iceberg algorithm* – based on the total execution of order by placing bids with a total maximum capacity no more than some predetermined value. Placing of orders should be continued till the total execution of order. This greatly improves the efficiency of the algorithm, since for its realization it is enough to put only one bid, which will be executed much faster than the number of sequentially exposed trading orders.

1.2) *Time Weighted Average Price (TWAP) algorithm* - implies the unified execution of the total amount of orders for the specified number of iterations during a specified period of time - by placing the market orders at prices better, than demand or supply price, adjusted for a given value of percentage deviation.

1.3) *Volume Weighted Average Price (VWAP) algorithm* - implies the unified execution of the total amount of orders for the specified number of iterations during a specified period of time - by placing the market orders at prices better, than demand or supply price, adjusted for a given value of percentage deviation, but not exceeding the weighted average market price of the security, designed from the start of the algorithm.

2) Speculative strategies

The main purpose of the speculative strategies is to get profit in the short term due to the "exploitation" of fluctuations in market prices of financial instruments. In order to classify them, experts distinguish seven main groups of speculative strategies, some of which use the principles and algorithms of other groups (Colby, 2002).

2.1) *Market-making strategy* - suggests the simultaneous offering and maintenance of buy and sell orders of financial instrument. These strategies use the principle of "random walk" in prices within the current trend, in other words, despite the rise in security price at a certain time interval, some part of transactions will lead to decrease the security/commodity prices, and vice-verse, in the case of a general fall in the price of the instrument, some part of transactions will result to increase its prices comparing with previous values. Thus, in the case of well-chosen buy and sell orders, it's possible to buy low and sell high, regardless of the current trend direction.

There are various models of determining of optimal price of orders, selection of which is based on the liquidity of instrument, the amount of funds placed in the strategy, the allowable time of holding position and other factors (Edwards, Magee, 2007).

The key factor in the success of this type of strategies is the maximization of compliance of quotations to the current market conditions for chosen instrument, which can be reached by high speed of obtaining the market data and the ability to change quickly the order's price, otherwise, these strategies become unprofitable.

Market-makers are among the main "suppliers" of instant liquidity, and at the expense of competition they help to improve the "liquidity profile". That is why stock exchange centers quite often try to attract market-makers in illiquid instruments, providing them with favorable conditions of the commissions, and in some cases, paying fees for the maintenance of prices.

2.2) *Trend following strategy* - based on the principle of identifying the trend on the time series of price values of financial instrument (using for that purpose a variety of technical indicators), and buying or selling an instrument with the appearance of corresponding signals (Colby, 2002).

A characteristic feature of trend following strategies is that they can be used on almost all time frames - from the tick to monthly, but because of the fact that profitability of these strategies depends on the ratio of correct to incorrect predictions about the future direction of price movements, it might be quite risky to use them on too large time frames, since an error of prediction usually can be detected after relatively long period of time – which can lead to serious losses.

The effectiveness of trend following strategies, especially in intra-day trading, depends mostly on the instantaneous liquidity of financial instrument, because most of transactions take place through the market orders at current prices of supply and demand. Therefore, if the financial instrument has a wide spread and the horizontal curve of instant liquidity, then even in the case of a large number of true predictions strategy can cause damage.

2.3) *Pairs trading strategy* - based on the analysis of price's relation of two highly correlated financial instruments. A key principle of pair trading strategies is the convergence property of the current price with its moving average. That is why in the case of deviation from the average ratio for a predetermined value, investor should buy a certain amount of first financial instrument and simultaneously sell another appropriate financial instrument. In the situation, when prices return to the average ratio, investor should execute the opposite transaction.

For the analysis of prices ratios usually can be used the same indicators of technical analysis, as for the analysis of trend following strategies. However, the convergence property of prices can be clearly expressed mostly at small time intervals, so for the analysis of pairs at large time intervals it is better to use the comparing indicators of fundamental analysis, such as market multiples, profitability ratios and financial ratios.

2.4) *Basket trading strategies* - repeat the principles underlying in the strategy of pair trading, with the only difference being that the price ratio is constructed for the two "baskets of instruments." The price of each basket is calculated based on the prices of several different instruments, taking into account the number of units of each financial instrument in the basket (Edwards, Magee, 2007).

Just as for the pair trading strategies, when the deviation of ratio of prices from its average meaning reaches a given – predetermined value, it is necessary to buy all the instruments included in the first basket and simultaneously to sell all the instruments included in another basket. When the ratio returns to the average meaning, it is necessary to make the opposite transaction. To analyze the relative prices of financial instrument's baskets, it is possible to use the same indicators of technical analysis, as for trend following strategies.

The effectiveness of basket trading strategies depends on the immediate liquidity of instruments, since almost all transactions are made through the market orders at current prices of supply and demand, and trade goes primarily intra-day. For these reasons, basket trading strategies are used mostly exclusively in highly liquid instruments.

2.5) *Arbitrage strategies* - most of them are a special case of the pair trading, with the only feature that the pair consists of similar or related assets with the correlation of almost equal to or close to 1. Consequently, the prices ratio of such instruments will often be almost unchangeable.

Arbitrage strategies conditionally can be divided into several types, based on the assets using for trading (McDonald, 2005):

Spatial arbitrage - involves the usage of completely identical instruments, but traded on different markets, such as: stocks in New York – stocks in London; futures in New York – futures in London;

Equivalent arbitrage - involves the usage of related financial instruments, when the price of one of the instruments is a linear combination of the price of another instrument, such as stock – futures;

Index arbitrage – based on the arbitraging of index futures price to a basket of instruments based on index.

Optional arbitrage - based on the principle of parity in the value of Put and Call options, in violation of which it is necessary to buy one type of option and simultaneously to sell another type of option. Also it's necessary to buy or sell the appropriate amount of the underlying asset.

The effectiveness of arbitrage strategies is highly dependent on the speed of receiving market data and the speed of placing orders that is why the arbitrage can be attributed to the most technologically advanced algorithms that require the presence of high-speed communication links and modern trade infrastructure.

2.6) *Low-latency trading strategies* - a modification of trend following strategies, but with the peculiarity that the trend is defined by one (baseline) financial instrument, and transactions are made on another (working) instrument.

The basic principle of these strategies is to use the properties of correlation between different financial instruments and delays in the dissemination of market information. Trend is usually identified on the small time frames for the instrument with a very high trading liquidity, since exactly these instruments play the role of drivers of price movements in the market and contribute to price changes in instruments with less liquidity.

When investor determined the direction of short-term trend in the "basic" instrument, then he\she sends market order for buying or selling the "working" instrument at the current price. In some cases, as a "working" instrument can be used more than one instrument – the basket from a variety of instruments, each of them has a high correlation coefficient with the "basic" instrument.

The effectiveness of low latency strategies is highly dependent on the speed of reception of market data for the "basic" instrument and the speed of placing orders on the "working" instrument that is why these strategies, as well as the arbitrage strategies, require high-speed communication links and modern trade infrastructure.

2.7) *Front running strategies* - based on an analysis of instant liquidity of the instrument and the average volume of transactions on the instrument within a certain time period.

If investor can find some market orders in the "area" close to the best bid and ask prices, and if the total volume of these orders exceeds the average volume of transactions over a certain time period on the specified value, then he\she should place the order in the same direction with price a little bit higher, than the price with average volume (in case of buying), or with price a little bit lower (in case of selling).

In this case the investor's order takes place before the orders with large volume, and if it executes, it's necessary to place the opposite order with the price a little bit higher (in case of initial buying) or a little bit lower (in case of initial selling). The main principle is based on the idea, that the high-volume orders will be executed over some period of time for which it will be possible to execute several deals in the opposite direction. It is believed that the front running strategies work best with the instruments with high trading liquidity, but their effectiveness depends primarily on the speed of receiving market data and speed of placing orders.

3.2 Index investment strategies. Literature and review of investing implementation

Depending on the volume of assets under management, timing of investment and risk-tolerance there are different types of investing strategies. They can be divided into *active* and *passive* (Ferri, 2002).

Active type involves the in-depth study of the financial condition of the issuer's, assessment of its value, as well as the interpretation of the numerous financial indicators. The best known methods are the discounting of cash flows, market multiples method, etc.

Passive type is based on a monitoring of current changes in the security's prices and actually usage the results of actively trading managers. One of the areas of passive investing is the so called index investing.

The principal difference between the index investing and the other investment strategies is that managers - in the first case - "do not make an effort to beat the market, but they try to follow it" (Passive Index Investment Strategies are Superior, 2007).

The results of indexing strategies can be quite impressive (in the situations of favorable market conditions and selecting appropriate time frames). But, as many experts emphasize, there are quite obvious risks (Tergesen, Young, 2004).

The theory of index investing was created in the fifties of the last century - during the interpretation of the results of the Great Depression. The prototype was the approach of "cross-section of markets", when the selectivity in the formation of the investment portfolio has given a way to the additional returns, based on specific portfolio characteristics. This method was considered as a quite effective way of investing in the long run (Sharpe, 1991).

Then Malkien (1973) defined that individual investors can achieve better results when they buy and hold the securities of index funds, which invest in the S&P 500, rather than when they buy and sell shares of individual companies.

The main argument for index investing is an obtaining of market returns combined with low costs of investing process. When the mutual funds returns were compared with the selected markets (for stocks in the US. the S&P 500 index is most commonly used) it was noted, that other methods of portfolio management do not always give stable results. And they do not always reach the results of the market returns! (Gibson, 2006)

Obviously, index funds do not have such a problem! The process of the index investing is fully computerized and it's held in automatic mode. Index funds do not generate cash reserves to overcome the trend reversal or a falling market. Due to the compounding effect of complex interest rate, these reserves can generate a high added value in long-term time intervals (Fabocci, 1995).

Many analysts (Pozen, Hamacher 2011) note the coincidence in time of beginning the broad usage of index funds based on the S&P 500 and beginning of the greatest upward trend on the US stock market. There is a perception that especially because of the dramatically increased popularity of index investments in the components of S&P 500 index, the whole market started to grow.

Due to increased public interest in the index investments during the market's growth, index investments contribute to the "self-empowerment" - the upward movement of market. This, in particular, is confirmed by a clear correlation between the increasing flows of investments in index funds in periods of market growth and the reduction of flows in the periods of market's fall.

In the 1990s because of the promising breakthrough in the field of information technology and the Internet there was a large number of inexperienced investors involved in the US. stock market. Faith of investors in an endless continuation of the uprising trend, ignorance the findings of fundamental analysis, following not the facts but opinions of the overwhelming majority have created an excessive demand for the securities that formed a giant "bubble." Investing in the end proved to be extremely dangerous, and brought substantial losses to investors (Naiman, 2004).

To be safe from such problems, index funds in the US. began to offer investors to diversify their investments. For example, to transfer funds in instruments that are not closely correlated with the S&P 500 (index investing in bonds, in funds that specialize in international stocks, securities of emerging market stocks of the US. companies with small capitalization, mortgage trusts and short-term instruments with a fixed income). Accordingly, the method of forming investing strategy has become more complex, the way of calculation returns has changed (Galitz, 2002).

A large variety of stock indexes and (established on their bases) index funds allow investors to effortlessly build diversified portfolio in accordance with their investment objective, risk tolerance and available resources. Some examples of the most popular stock indexes/sub-indexes, like general market/sector and international are listed in Table 2.

Table 2. Some of the indexes/sub-indexes which are used for forming index investment strategies

Market segment	Index/Sub-index
Broad the U.S. market	Wilsgire 5000 Equity Index
Large capitalization stocks	S&P 500 – Composite Stock Price Index; FTSE Global Equity Index Series (FTSE All-World); FTSE UK Index Series (FTSE 100, FTSE 250, FTSE All-Share); DAX 30; CAC 40;
Large capitalization value stocks	S&P 500 – BARRA Value Index
Large capitalization growth stocks	S&P 500 – BARRA Growth Index
Mid-capitalization stocks	S&P 500 - MidCap 400 Index
Small and middle capitalization stocks	Wilshire 4500 Equity Index
Small capitalization stocks	Russel 2000 Index
Small capitalization value stocks	S&P SmallCap 600/BARRA Value Index
Small capitalization growth stocks	S&P SmallCap 600/BARRA Growth Index
Major non-US stocks	Morgan Stanley Capital International Europe, Australasia, Far East (EAFE) Index
European stocks	Morgan Stanley Capital International Europe Index (sub-index of EAFE)
Pacific Region stocks	Morgan Stanley Capital International Pacific Free Index (sub-index of EAFE)
Stocks in emerging markets in Asia, Latin America and Europe	Morgan Stanley Capital International Select Emerging Markets Free Index

Source: http://www.vunt.ru/etfunds/table1.htm

Comparing with the passive investment strategies, active strategies have the weakness "of bad choice". According to O'Neal (1997) there is a 12 to 1 ratio for the best performing mutual fund compared to the worst performing mutual fund over a 19-year period from 1976 to 1994. If investor makes the wrong choices in selection, then wider variability of returns can subject him\her to far greater risks comparing with passive market index strategy.

Also, Bernstein (2000) shows that randomly chosen stock portfolios will under-perform the market return. The primary reason is that stocks with high long-term returns are relatively few in number and are not obvious choices before the fact. Therefore, more portfolios will not contain them and thus will under-perform the market average.

But, it is worth of mentioning some weaknesses of passive investments too: for example, the high dependence of stock indexes from major companies. In the U.S. the estimated base of the S&P 500 consists of 500 leading shares of companies belonging to leading industries. These are very large companies, and the percentage of their shares in the index is weighted by their market capitalization. Shares of small and medium-sized companies remain outside the S&P 500. Therefore, if just a few large companies will fail, the result for the investor would be extremely negative.

There is couple of ways to solve this problem (Gibson, 2006):

1) *The usage of more extensive index.*

For example, the Wilshire 5000, that includes the vast majority of the shares of companies, listed on the U.S. exchanges (the Fund Vanguard Total Stock Market Index). However, since weighting is based on the market capitalization of its components, the problem partially remained.

2) *The usage of index based on equal weights*

The usage of S&P 500 model, but when the share of each issuer does not exceed 0.2%. During the years of falling market investments loses much smaller.

But there are also some negative factors of such model of index:

- high volatility of small capitalization stocks, and hence risk;
- high turnover of the portfolio (with a monthly review to bring the share of each share to 0.2%) and, consequently, high costs;

Also some experts (Naiman, 2004) show that the usage of index strategies can lead to another problem: the inclusion/exclusion of the issuer's securities to/from the index to which large amounts of index investments linked, lead to change the prices of these securities without any other fundamental changes in the position of the issuer.

3.2.1 The main types of index investment strategies

1) Capitalization weight

Traditional stock market index is calculated by the stock price of "basket", where each equity has a certain weight. The latter depends on the company's market capitalization relative to the total capitalization of all companies included in the index. The larger the capitalization of the company, the more it has an effect on the index (Galitz, 2002).

This classical approach emerged extensively in the first half of the 20th century, when it was believed that the market knows and takes into account all the fundamentals, which is reflected in the capitalization and trading volume - liquidity. "Positive aspect of this interpretation is that the high liquidity of the shares allows to reduce transaction costs of investors, which in turn leads to the effect of "scalability" - when the yield of the portfolio is almost independent of the volume of investment" (Gibson, 2006).

The latter circumstance is the reason, that in the modern world, index strategies are used for the largest part of the assets. At the same time, it is clear that many companies with high capitalization is fundamentally overvalued at the expense of less capitalized companies that will likely continue to be undervalued.

2) Fundamental indexing

The absence of any apparent relationship between the financial performance of companies and the weight in the index, and the recognition of the fact, that markets are inefficient, have led to the emergence of fundamental indexing. This principle has been proposed in 2005 by researchers of *Research Affiliates LLC.* The main idea of this method is that the weight of each stock in the index is determined by the fundamentals of company: shareholders' equity from the last reporting date (book value), the average sales over the past five years, the average value of cash flows over the past five years and the average amount of dividends over the past five years. An abbreviated form of this approach is called *RAFI (Research Affiliates Fundamental Indexing).*

The largest index agencies have already started to count RAFI-indexes, and this trend becomes more pronounced. However, there are some disadvantages of fundamental indexing (Gibson, 2006): indexes are calculated based on historical rather than projected financial performance and therefore do not account for future changes. In other words, there is a risk that companies, which have shown brilliant financial results in the past, will receive a high weight in the index, but their future may be very vague.

3) Equal-weighted indexing

The third type of recognized index strategy - is an equal weighting strategy (EWI). According to this type, all the stocks in the index have the same weight. Moreover, a set of shares for the calculation of EWI-index coincides with the set of the official stock exchange index. "It is believed that by using an index, the investor does not want to predict the future and rely on chance" (Gibson, 2006). This is a very simple principle, but it might be effective: historical data indicate that EWI-indices generate substantially higher returns, especially on a long interval.

A disadvantage of this approach is that transaction costs in the stock market are lower when we use capitalized and fundamental indexes. Hence, EWI-indexes begin to show lower results with increasing the amount of the investment portfolio. It's possible to say that the scalability of these indexes is limited. Despite this, EWI-indexes approach is a very actively used in the futures markets, where there are a lot of calculations of "currency basket" or a "basket of goods"(Tolstousov, 2010).

4) Risk-based indexation/minimal variance

The fourth approach of indexing strategies bases on the principle of reducing overall portfolio risk (risk-based indexation, or a minimal variance, then-RBI) (Tolstousov, 2010).

In this case, the weight of each stock depends on the individual risk: the higher the risk, the lower the weight. An advantages of the RBI-index is that in the long time interval, it has a very high Sharpe ratio, and low volatility (that is why, for example, such a strategy is primarily of interest to pension funds). At the same time there is a potential significant problem: the investor has to go beyond the official index, because it's necessary to find stocks with the minimal risk.

The world's leading index agencies have been realized that large institutional investors require standardized index products for the development of different strategies. For example, the agency Standard & Poor's (together with the official index of the broad market S&P 500) calculates the equal weighted index S&P 500 EWI. The family of FTSE indexes (Financial Times Agency) along with the official FTSE 100 also includes a fundamental index FTSE RAFI UK 100 Index. In fact, almost all capitalized indexes from S&P and FTSE have alternative counterparts on the basis of RAFI-and EWI-methodologies.

More detailed information about the indexes, which are used in this paper (including detailed specification of indexes), can be found in Appendix 1.

4 Empirical Methodology

4.1 Exponential moving average with a variable factor of smoothing

The dynamics of the movement of asset prices is characterized by the fact that at any given time there are more or less defined trend and noise components. The purpose of smoothing the price series is to filter the noise fluctuations in order to identify trends in sustainable movement. In an ideal moving average (MA), the maximum smoothing of noise must be combined with minimal distortion of trends (Sherry, 1992).

However, it is obvious that these two conditions are contradictory. In addition, the case is complicated by the fact that the characteristics of trends and noise are irregular in time. Therefore, for smoothing (at each point in time) it is necessary to maintain a reasonable balance between the measure of smoothness and the measure of proximity of the MA to the original price range, and this balance must correspond to the current price dynamics.

One of the most popular methods for smoothing is the exponential moving average (EMA). The method of its calculation is as follows (Pring, 2002).

Let's introduce the following notation:

- $\{X_t\}$ - series of prices (or the logarithm of the price) of the asset

- $\{Y_t\}$ - moving average of series $\{X_t\}$.

As a measure of proximity of the series $\{X_t\}$ and $\{Y_t\}$ at time t let's choose the function $(Xt - Yt)^2$, and as a measure of the smoothness of the series Y_t function $(Y_t - Y_{(t-1)})^2$.

If we take a weighted sum of these functions, i.e.

$$\Delta S_t = w \cdot (X_t - Y_t)^2 + (1-w) \cdot (Y_t - Y_{(t-1)})^2$$

then to calculate the present value of Yt, which minimizes the function Δs_t, it is necessary to solve the following equation:

$$\frac{\partial \Delta st}{\partial Yt} = 0$$

Solving it, we see that:

$$Y_t = Y_{(t-1)} + w \cdot (X_t - Y_{(t-1)})$$

This is the formula for the classical EMA with a constant smoothing factor w. Usually trading algorithms based on the EMA gives the signal to buy/sales the asset by changing the sign of the first derivative or first difference, i.e. the value

$$\Delta Y_t = Y_t - Y_{(t-1)}$$

According to Bulashev (2010) "the obvious disadvantage of EMA is it's constancy in the smoothing factor. The formula for its calculation does not take into account that the characteristics of trends and noise are irregular in time. Therefore, when a smoothing is large (small w), EMA provides little false signals to buy/sell on the flat, but it signals about the change in trend very late in time. In contrast, in case of a weak smoothing (large w), EMA reacts with a slight delay in change in trend, but it generates a lot of false alarms in the flat."

Bulashev (2010) offers one of the possible methods of calculating the EMA with time-varying smoothing factor that adapts to the dynamics of the current price.

The adaptation consists in the fact that the more obvious trend component in price is, the higher value the smoothing factor should take, that will reduces the delay of the moving average of the price.

In contrast, in the flat market conditions the smoothing factor should decrease, while the moving average becomes a horizontal (or nearly horizontal) line.

In some calculations (for details, see the reference), Bulashev finds that the formula for calculating the moving average should take form:

$$Y_t = Y_{(t-1)} + w_t \cdot \left(X_t - Y_{(t-1)} \right)$$

where

$$W_t = W_{min} + (W_{max} - W_{min}) \cdot \left(1 - e^{\left(-\left| \frac{X_t - Y_{(t-1)}}{E} \right|^a \right)} \right)$$

Formally, the algorithm for calculating the moving average (EMAVFS) has 4 parameters:

- W_{min} and W_{max} limit the range of variation of W_t,

- a describes the dependency of wt from approximation error

$$\delta_t = X_t - Y_{(t-1)}$$

- E determines the sensitivity of wt to the changes in error

$$\delta_t = X_t - Y_{(t-1)}$$

However, in practice, some of these parameters do not necessarily should be used as variables to be optimized.

For example, it's quite logical to set W_{min} apriori equal to 0. Shape parameter a after some research, can also be fixed at some level. As a result, only the upper limit W_{max} and the parameter of sensitivity E should be variables for optimization.

Further Bulashev (2010) shows, that, in fact, EMA algorithm with variable smoothing factor depends only on the single parameter E (or $\Delta Smax$):

Wt - parameter of smoothing can be defined as:

$$W_t = 0{,}5 \cdot (1 - \sqrt{1 - Z_t^2})$$

if $0 \leq Zt \leq 1$ (i.e. $\left| X_t - Y_{(t-1)} \right| \leq E$) and

$$W_t = 0{,}5 \cdot (1 - \sqrt{1 - \frac{1}{Z_t^2}})$$

if $1 < Zt \leq \infty$ (i.e. $\left| X_t - Y_{(t-1)} \right| \geq E$)

$$Z_t = \left| \frac{X_t - Y_{(t-1)}}{E} \right|$$

Calculated by this algorithm, the variable of smoothing factor Wt can be substituted into the formula for calculating the EMA:

$$Y_t = Y_{(t-1)} + w_t \cdot (X_t - Y_{(t-1)})$$

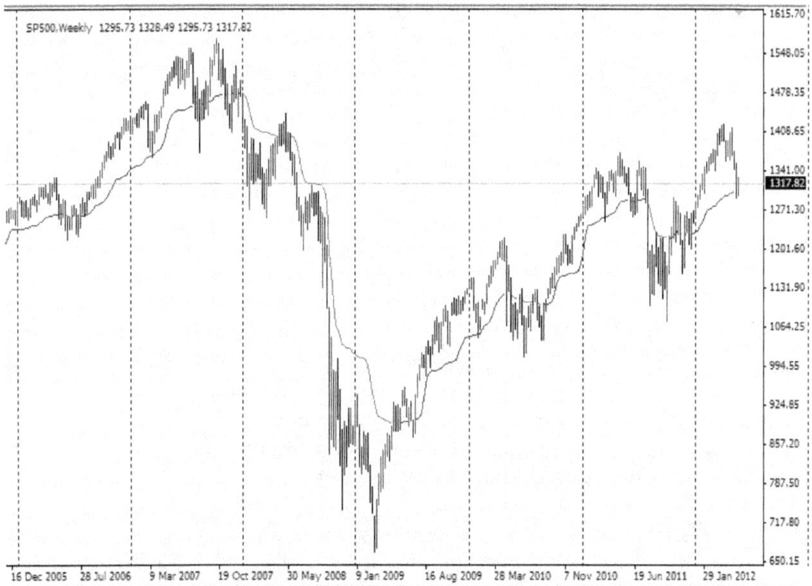

Figure 8. Exponential Moving Average with a Variable Factor of Smoothing
Source: Own calculations

Exactly this trading strategy based on EMAVFS indicator, I will analyze in this paper, for which it's necessary to develope a trading robot that generates trading signals based on the algorithm described above. The code of this trading robot (for platform Meta Language Quote 4) can be found in Appendix 2.

4.2 Statistical Arbitrage in High-Frequency Trading

One of the most popular and wildly used trading strategies among high-frequency trading "group" is the strategy of statistical arbitrage between futures on some market index and the spot value of this index. In reaction on the macroeconomic news, political announcements, business reports of companies and some other factors, futures markets response more quickly than spot markets.

Kawaller, Koch, and Koch (1993), for example, show that prices of the S&P 500 futures react to news faster than prices of the S&P500 index itself, in the Granger causality specification. A similar effect was documented by Stoll and Whaley (1990): for returns measured in 5-minute intervals, both S&P 500 and money market index futures led stock market returns by 5 to 10 minutes.

Mathematical foundations of statistical arbitrage were demonstrated very effectively by Aldridge (2009). According to her "the statistical arbitrage signals are based on a relationship between price levels or other variables characterizing any two securities." In more details the connection between price levels $S_{i,t}$ and $S_{j,t}$ for any two financial instruments i and j can be shown like that:

1) Define two (or more) financial instruments with good enough liquidity for trading with settled frequency.

2) "Measure the difference between prices of every two securities, i and j, identified in step (1) across time t:

$$Sij,t = Si,t - Sj,t, \ t \in [1,T]$$

where T is a sufficiently large number of daily observations. According to the central limit theorem (CLT) of statistics, 30 observations at selected trading frequency constitute the bare minimum. The intra-day data, however, has high seasonality — that is, persistent relationships can be observed at specific hours of the day. Thus, a larger T of at least 30 daily observations is strongly recommended. For robust inferences, a T of 500 daily observations (two years) is desirable" Aldridge (2009).

3) For each pair of financial instruments it's necessary to define the most stable relationship – to find securities that move together. To do this, Gatev, Goetzmann, and Rouwenhorst (2006) perform a simple minimization of the historical differences in returns between every two liquid securities:

$$min \sum_{t=1}^{T} \left(\Delta S_{ij,t} \right)^2$$

4) Estimate the main statistical properties of the difference as follows:

Mean or average of the difference:

$$E[\varDelta S_t] = \frac{1}{T} \sum_{t=1}^{T} (\varDelta S_t)$$

Standard deviation:

$$\sigma[\varDelta S_t] = \frac{1}{T-1} \sum_{t=1}^{T} (\varDelta S_t - E[\varDelta S_t])^2$$

5) Monitor and act upon differences in security prices:

At a particular time τ, if

$$\varDelta S_\tau = S_{i,\tau} - S_{j,\tau} > E[\varDelta S_\tau] + 2\sigma[\varDelta S_\tau]$$

sell security i and buy security j. On the other hand, if

$$\varDelta S_\tau = S_{i,\tau} - S_{j,\tau} < E[\varDelta S_\tau] - 2\sigma[\varDelta S_\tau]$$

buy security i and sell security j.

6) Once the gap in security prices reverses to achieve a desirable gain, close out the positions. If the prices move against the predicted direction, activate stop loss.

The algorithm described above I will use for developing the second trading robot for algorithmic trading. The code of this trading robot (for platform Meta Language Quote 4) can be found in Appendix 2.

4.3 Organization of trading infrastructure. Development of trading robots

Development a high-frequency trading system is a quite different process comparing with other traditional financial businesses. As Aldridge (2009, p.27) states "designing new high-frequency trading strategies is very costly; executing and monitoring finished high-frequency products costs close to nothing. By contrast, traditional proprietary trading businesses incur fixed costs from the moment an experienced senior trader with a proven track record begins running the trading desk and training promising young apprentices, through the time when the trained apprentices replace their masters."

According to Aldgridge (2009, p.28) "the cost of traditional trading remains fairly constant through time. With the exception of trader "burn-outs" necessitating hiring and training new trader staff, costs of staffing the traditional trading desk do not change. Developing computerized trading systems, however, requires an up-front investment that is costly in terms of labor and time. One successful trading system takes on average 18 months to develop. The costs of computerized trading decline as the system moves into production, ultimately requiring a small support staff that typically includes a dedicated systems engineer and a performance monitoring agent. Both the systems engineer and a monitoring agent can be responsible for several trading systems simultaneously, driving the costs closer to zero."

Among all the factors making the influence on the effectiveness of algorithmic trading, the question of elaboration of technical organization of trading algorithm takes one of the most important places. The way of connection the trading terminal, which generates trading signals for buying and selling, and the "core" of the corresponding stock exchange center, the speed of reception of market data - are the critical factors in determining the profitability.

Generally, the time-dependent flow of the order execution process can be illustrated on Figure 9.

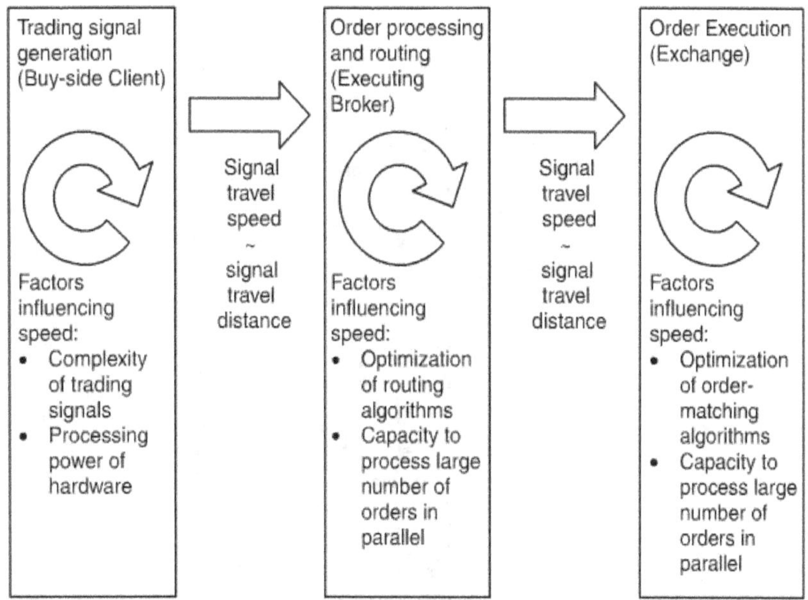

Figure 9. Order execution process

Source: Aldridge, I., 2009, *High-Frequency Trading: A Practical Guide to Algorithmic Strategies and Trading Systems, John Wiley & Sons*, p.246

To understand the problem of "signal travel speed" let's consider the example of Serebryanikov (2011) for organizing the connection to the RTS-FORTS (Futures and Options section of Russian Trading System).

In the Figure 10 there are the following variants of connection:

Variant A is the most economical among all existing, because basically there is no need for any extra cost, except the payment for software for algorithmic trading (trading robot), which is, in principle, can be coded by investor/trader.

The disadvantages of this variant is the biggest delay in the receiving of market data and the lowest speed of placing trading orders, which is associated with a large number of intermediate links between trading terminal and core of trading system FORTS.

Besides that, there are numbers of external risks that may cause instability of the algorithmic system, such as interruption of the Internet connection or a failed brokerage system. Taking this into account, this variant is not recommended for making real deals in the high-frequency trading.

Approximate cost of this variant is varying from 200 USD to 1700 USD, depending on the price of software for algorithmic trading implementation.

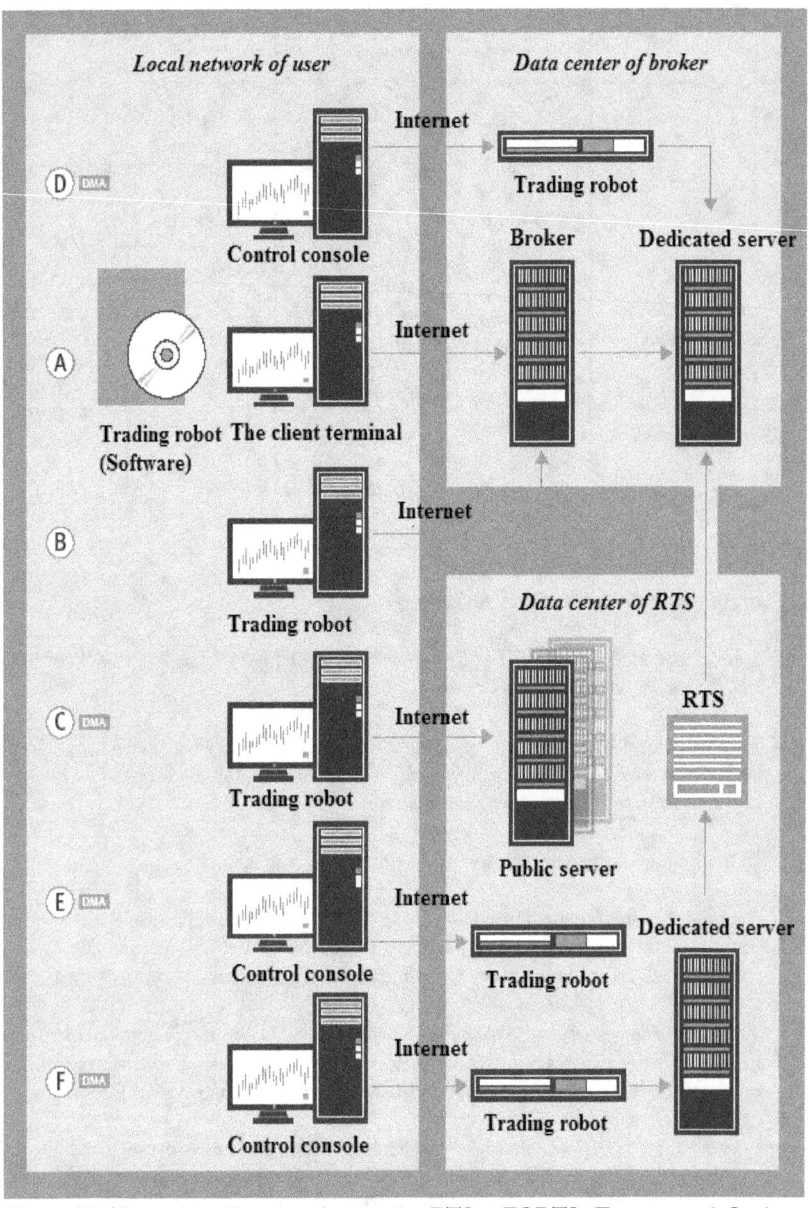

Figure 10. The ways of connection to the RTS – FORTS (Futures and Options section of Russian Trading System)

Source: Serebryannikov, D. (2011). Introduction to algorithmic trading, *Journal of Futures & Options*, no.4

Variant B is almost identical to the previous with the only difference that the connection to broker system does not require the presence of the trading terminal.

Despite the exclusion of one intermediary, this version of access to market is not very different in delay the data, speed of placing the orders and external risks from the *Variant A*, which is also limits its usage for high-frequency trading.

Variants C, D, E and *F* are form group of Direct Market Access (DMA) technologies. They are characterized by direct connecting the trading robot with the stock exchange trading infrastructure, in this case to an intermediate server of FORTS. In connection with the minimum number of units, DMA is the best solution for high-frequency algorithmic trading systems.

Let's consider each DMA variant in more detail.

Variant C – is the easiest to implement and the most economical variant among DMA. All expenses are limited by payment for the software and access to server through which trading robot receives the market data and exposes the orders.

This variant is much better than the *Variant A* and *B*, but it has one important disadvantage of using the Internet connection to communicate with the stock trading infrastructure. The thing is, that the connection over the Internet does not guarantee the quality of data, since on the "path" from the trading robot to stock exchange infrastructure there are a lot of routers, each of which may have a queue of data packets, resulting in a significant reduction in the speed of transmission of data or it's loss.

The price of this variant includes the cost of software (from 200 till 1700 USD) and the access to server. The minimum cost of access to server of FORTS is 2360 rubles (approximately 80 USD). per month, but the real price will depend on the selected number of authorized transactions per second and brokerage.

Variant D allows eliminating of risks associated with the Internet connection, through the transfer of market data over a dedicated internet channel that provides a stable speed of connection with minimal losses.

To do this, it's necessary to place trading robot in the data-center of broker, which involves additional costs for the purchasing of hardware (server) for trading robot and server location in data-center (approximate price of it is from 200 USD). But this variant of market access is already suitable for connecting professional algorithmic trading systems.

Despite of all the advantages of this variant, there is still a number of external risks from the common usage of the selected channel by all the clients of broker - that can lead to "clogging" of the selected channel or server overload.

Variant E allows to eliminate the risk associated with a dedicated communication channel, and to achieve minimum delays in the reception of market data by placing trading robot in the data-center RTS. However, the maximum proximity to the exchange trading infrastructure will require additional expenses, including payment for receiving data from the RTS network and the Internet access for remote management trading robot.

Variant F is considered as the most reliable and efficient among all the existing variants because of elimination of the last external risk from using the server by groups of traders. The implementation of this variant would require the cost of hardware for a server, purchasing license and installation of the software for server, as well as the services of its location in the data-center RTS. The price of this service is from 2000 till 4000 USD (all the prices here are actual for the beginning of 2011).

However, in this study, I will use ***Variant B***, as the most simple in terms of modeling and financial cost.

According to Aldgridge (2009, p.234) "the development of a fully automated trading system follows a path similar to that of the standard software development process."

The typical life cycle of a development process is illustrated in Figure 11.

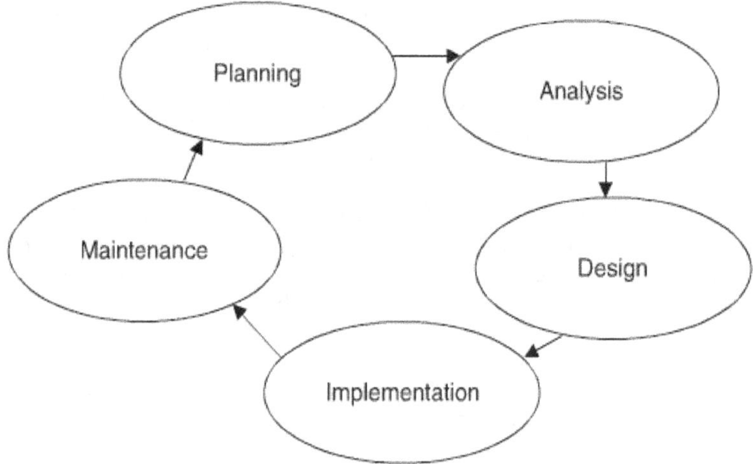

Figure 11. Typical development cycle of a trading system

Source: Aldridge, I., 2009, *High-Frequency Trading: A Practical Guide to Algorithmic Strategies and Trading Systems, John Wiley & Sons*, p.234

"A sound development process normally consists of the following five phases." Aldgridge (2009, p.234):

1. Planning
2. Analysis
3. Design
4. Implementation

5. Maintenance

In functional terms, experts (Aldridge, 2009) suppose that "most systematic trading platforms are organized in a way, according to which one or several run-time processors contain the core logic of the trading mechanism and perform the following functions:
1) Receive, evaluate, and archive incoming quotes
2) Perform run-time econometric analysis
3) Implement run-time portfolio management
4) Initiate and transmit buy and sell trading signals
5) Listen for and receive confirmation of execution
6) Calculate run-time Profit & Lose
7)Dynamically manage risk based on current portfolio allocations and market conditions."

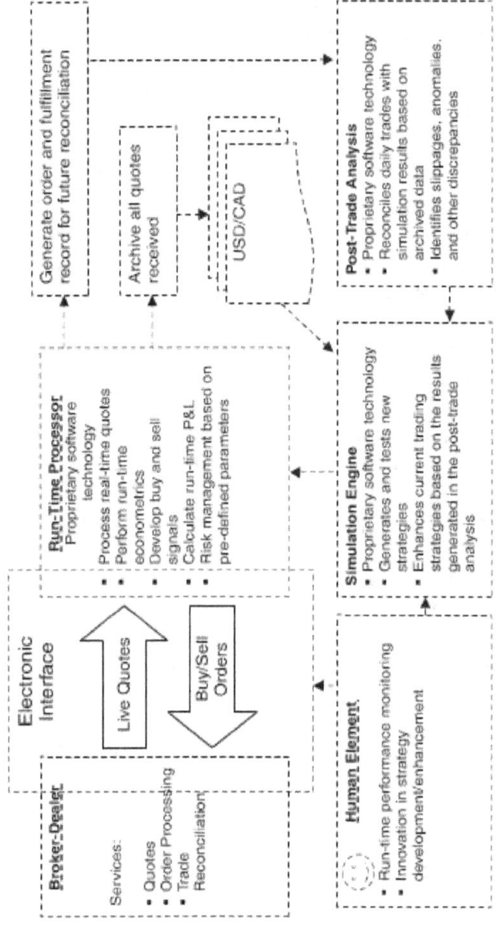

Figure 12. Typical high-frequency process.
Source: Aldridge, I., 2009, *High-Frequency Trading: A Practical Guide to Algorithmic Strategies and Trading Systems, John Wiley & Sons*, p.237

5. Empirical results and analysis

5.1 Data.

For this study analysis, there were chosen three stock market indexes:

1) S&P 500 (the U.S. index of "broad market")
2) FTSE 100 (the UK) - *since these two markets are ones of the biggest in capitalization and most liquid (and, for this reason, most "efficient" in terms of the Efficient Market Hypothesis)*
3) OMX Stockholm 30 Index (Sweden) - *in order to check whether the Swedish stock market acts as well as its larger global counterparts.*

Though, the first trading algorithms appeared on American markets in the middle of 1980s, they became significantly popular in the mid/late 1990s, since till that moment all the advantages of information technology's "boom" (widely usage of the Internet and personal computers, developing of trading software applications with user-friendly interface, and so on) were implemented by equity's trading.

That is why, from the first look, it would be logical to choose the middle of 1990s – as an initial point for my research. But, taking into consideration several crises, which happened in the late of 1990s (Asian crisis (1997), Russian crisis (1998), Argentinean crisis (2000-2001) and "DotCom bubble" crisis in the U.S. (2000 – 2003)) and effected world stock markets a lot (for ex., S&P 500 lost 50% of its' capitalization from the peak 1551.76 in March of 2000, till the bottom of 768.65 in October of 2002 – see Figure 13), it would be logical to choose another initial point, because all the index investing strategies from 1998 till 2003 would show negative returns.

In contrast, index investing strategies could show very high positive returns from the period of 01.01.2003 till 01.11.2007, and from 01.03.2009 till 01.05.2012 (see Figure 14). That is why, it is more logical to compare algorithmic trading with a very "successful alternative" – index strategies on periods, when they could get high returns.

So, to make the results of study more relevant, I considered the period of time from 01.01.2003 to 01.01.2012, when the previous crisis of 2001-2002 (the "DotCom bubble") has been overcome, but, nevertheless, I considered the period of crisis 2007-2009 too, because of increase in volatility (since it strongly effects the returns of index strategies).

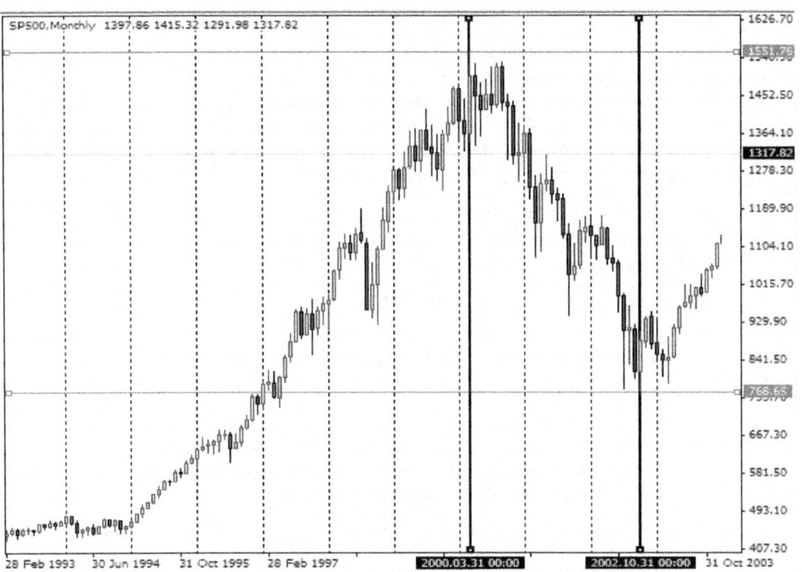

Figure 13. The falling of S&P 500 in the late 1990s – beginning of 2000s.
Source: Own calculations

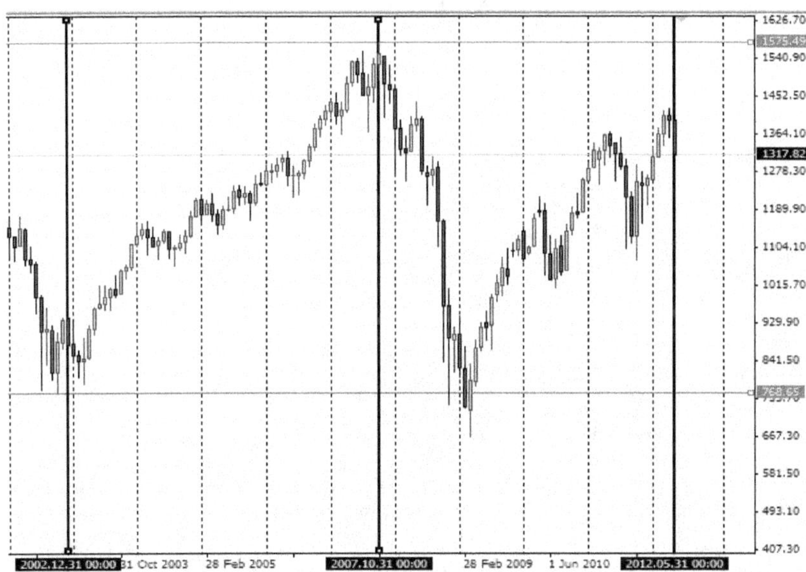

Figure 14. Significant Up-trends on S&P 500 from 01.01.2003 till 01.11.2007 and from 01.03.2009 till 01.05.2012
Source: Own calculations

5.2 Observation, calculations and results of index strategies' performing

To make the correct conclusion about the effectiveness of algorithmic trading strategies, it is necessary for us to get the correct benchmark, which we can use for comparison.

As it is described before in the section 3.2.1, in this study I used 4 different possible benchmarks:
   1) Capitalization weight index
   2) Fundamental indexing
   3) Equal-weighted indexing
   4) Risk-based indexation/minimal variance

For all of these types of indexes I collected the data and calculated returns for considered period of time.

Table 3 presents the results of calculations of the annual returns of indexes and their "total return" for the period under review. The period of observation: 01.01.2003 - 01.01.2012 (but as some indexes - FTSE 100 EWI, FTSE RAFI UK 100, FTSE 100 MVI - were invented later, their results are not for all the years from this period).

Detailed calculations of returns for all of the indexes can be found in Table A. 1 in Appendix 3.

Table 3. The ranking of indexes' returns for 01.01.2003 – 01.01.2012

№	Index	Total returns for all considered time, %
1	OMX Stockholm 30 Index	96.12
2	S&P 500 EWI	88.6
3	S&P 500	42.5
4	FTSE 100	39.13
5	FTSE 100 MVI	4,5
6	FTSE 100 EWI	-1.32
7	FTSE RAFI UK 100	-14.55

Source: Own calculations

As we can see the greatest returns for the period were shown by OMX Stockholm 30 Index, followed by the S&P 500 EWI with 88.6% and then - S&P 500 with 42.5%. The underperformance of strategies *Minimum Variance Index* and *RAFI* is not quite indicative in this case, because the FTSE 100 MVI and FTSE 100 EWI were launched only in December 23, 2011 - that is, the period of its' observation - 6 months - is much shorter than the period for other instruments. The same situation is with the index FTSE RAFI UK 100, which was launched only in 2007. Perhaps in a situation where these indexes are considered during 9 years, the results may be different. All the graphs of indexes for considering period of time can be found in Appendix 4.

5.3 Observation, calculations and results of algorithmic trading strategies

To test the effectiveness of algorithmic trading strategies, I have developed two trading robot on the inner programming language of trading platform - MetaQuotes Language 4 - using the algorithms described above in Sections 4.1 and 4.2 (The code data of trading robots can be found in the Appendix 2).

Programs written in MetaQuotes Language 4 have different features and purposes:

Expert Advisor

A mechanical trading system (MTS) linked up to a certain chart. An Advisor starts to run with every incoming tick for a given symbol. The Advisor will not be launched for a new, tick if it is processing the previous one at this moment (i.e., the Advisor has not completed its operation yet). The Advisor can both inform you about a possibility to trade and trade at an account automatically sending orders directly to the trade server. Like most trading systems, the terminal supports testing strategies on history data with displaying trading in-and-out points in the chart.

Custom Indicator

A technical indicator written independently in addition to those already integrated into the client terminal. Like built-in indicators, they cannot trade automatically and are intended for implementing of analytical functions only.

Script

A program intended for a single execution of some actions.
Unlike Expert Advisors, Scripts are not run tickwise, but on request

Library

A set of custom functions containing programs most frequently used. Libraries cannot start execution by itself.

Included file

A source text of the most frequently used blocks of custom programs. Such files can be included into the source texts of experts, scripts, custom indicators, and libraries at the compiling stage. The use of included files is more preferable than the use of libraries because of additional burden occurring at calling library functions.

Figure 15. Elements of program in MQL4
Source: http://docs.mql4.com/

When trading robots were developed, I connected them to the trading terminal installed on my computer (*trading terminal* is, basically, software, that broker provide you with). After that, all the historical quotes which I was interested in (for all the considered financial instruments, for all considered period of time, and for all needed time dimensions) were downloaded from the server of broker, and from that moment could be used in strategies' tester in trading terminal (the way of connection of trading robot with trading server is just like Variant B in Figure 4 in Section 4.3).

Using the trading robots, I tested historical quotes of three indexes (S& P500, FTSE100 and OMX Stockholm 30 Index) on the time interval from 01.01.2003 to 01.01.2012 in different "time dimensions": 5 minutes, 15 minutes, 1 hour, 4 hours, one day. Thus, for each of the selected stock market indexes, we have the opportunity to see at what "market phase" (year) and in which "time dimension» (M5, M15, H1, H4, D1) robot trading strategy would show the most successful results, and then to compare these results with the results of the passive (index) trading strategies.

Now let's try to analyze the test results of trading robots in various time frames in the selected time period from 01.01.2003 to 01.01.2012 for each of the three stock market indexes (S&P 500, FTSE 100, OMX Stockholm 30 Index).

Test results - average returns for all the period of observation - are presented in Table 4. More detailed calculations for every index can be found in Table A.2., Table A.3. and Table A.4. in Appendix 3.

Table 4. The average returns of trading robots for all the period of observation

Name of trading robot	Expert1					Expert 2				
Time frame / INDEX	M5	M15	H1	H4	D1	M5	M15	H1	H4	D1
S&P 500	-9.78	-10.4	11.14	28.49	-10.4	131.2	6.59	2.48	1.58	0.57
FTSE 100	-9.64	-7.61	8	14.26	-6.57	91.69	4.39	1.95	1.56	0.29
OMX Stockholm 30 Index	-8.34	-6.54	6.53	7.57	-4.21	92.64	3.49	1.98	0.87	0.79

Source: Own calculations

5.4 Results discussion

The purpose of this study is an attempt to check, if algorithmic trading can be more effective, than passive investing strategy. Namely, can algorithmic trading get the bigger returns, than index? What should investor do: to develop the trading robots and create appropriate informational and trading infrastructure in a hope to "outperform the market", or it is enough just to get average market return, corresponding with the average market risk?

Connected to the main purpose, there were formulated the set of research questions, which this thesis should have made more clear.

In the end, based on the analysis of results tables, it is possible to come to the following important conclusions:

1) *Which investing strategies – algorithmic trading or investing in index – could bring bigger returns to investors for period from 01.01.2003 to 01.01.2012?*

The returns of algorithmic trading and index investing strategies for each of the stock market indexes are presented in Table 5.

Table 5 Returns of algorithmic trading and index investing strategies for the indexes: S&P 500, FTSE 100, OMX Stockholm 30 Index

INDEX	Investing strategy (returns in %)	
	Algorithmic trading (with the name of corresponding robot and time frame)	**Index investing** (with the name of corresponding index)
S&P 500	131.19 (Expert2, M5) 28.49 (Expert1, H4)	88.6 (S&P 500 EWI) 42.5 (S&P 500)
FTSE 100	91.69 (Expert2, M5) 14.26 (Expert1, H4)	39.13 (FTSE 100)
OMX Stockholm 30 Index	92.64 (Expert2, M5)	96.12

Source: Own calculations

> As we can see, for **S&P 500** the biggest returns were shown by algorithmic trading (with *statistic arbitrage strategy*), then index investing (with *equal-weighted indexing* and *capitalization weight index* versions) is following, and then – algorithmic trading (with *trend-following strategy*).
> For **FTSE 100**, once again, there is a superiority of algorithmic trading (with *statistic arbitrage strategy*), then index investing (with *capitalization weight index* version) is following, and then – algorithmic trading (with *trend-following strategy*).
> For **OMX Stockholm 30 Index** the returns of different strategies are approximately equal (with a slight superiority for the index strategy).

Thus, we can say that:

at the current phase of markets' development, it is theoretically possible for algorithmic trading (and especially high-frequency strategies) to exceed the returns of index strategy, but we should note two important factors:

1) Taking into account all of the costs of organization of high-frequency trading (brokerage and stock exchanges commissions, trade-related infrastructure maintenance, etc.), the difference in returns (with superiority of high-frequency strategy) will be much less!

2) Given the fact that "markets' efficiency" is growing every year (see further about it), and the returns of high-frequency strategies tends to decrease with time (see further about it), it is quite logical to assume that it will be necessary to invest more and more in trading infrastructure to "fix" the returns of high-frequency trading strategies on a higher level, than the results of index investing strategies.

2) Which investing strategies – algorithmic trading or investing in index – got bigger returns in the period of crisis 2007-2009?

Table 6 Performance of index strategies during crisis 2007 - 2009

	Time Period	Indexes						
		S&P 500	S&P 500 EWI	FTSE 100	FTSE 100 EWI	FTSE RAFI UK 100	FTSE 100 MVI	OMX Stockholm 30 Index
Returns to the previous period, %	01.01.2007	9.8	13.34	12.31	Did not exist at that time	0	Did not exist at that time	20.8
Returns to the previous period, %	01.01.2008	3.53	-1.65	1.67	Did not exist at that time	3.7	Did not exist at that time	-9.1
Returns to the previous period, %	01.01.2009	-38.37	-43.84	-28.91	Did not exist at that time	-34.24	Did not exist at that time	-34.44

Source: Own calculations

Table 7 Returns of algorithmic trading strategies during crisis 2007 - 2009

INDEX	S&P 500									
Name of trading robot	Expert1					Expert 2				
Time Frame	M5	M15	H1	H4	D1	M5	M15	H1	H4	D1
Year	2007					2007				
Profit. (%)	-13.9	-12.7	14.22	11.71	-13.7	121.6	5.89	1.72	1.7	0.29
Year	2008					2008				
Profit. (%)	-14.1	-15.4	-17.9	-12.9	-12.9	95.15	4.18	3.14	1.44	0.66
Year	2009					2009				
Profit. (%)	-11.79	-3.24	-7.61	15.35	-14.3	98.49	12.17	2.97	1.48	0.14
INDEX	FTSE 100									
Year	2007					2007				
Profit. (%)	-7.13	-7.05	5.62	11.26	-8.86	101.2	3.48	2.37	1.64	0.34
Year	2008					2008				
Profit. (%)	-15.8	-11.1	-13.3	-14.8	-7.04	77.38	2.22	2.18	1.41	0.11
Year	2009					2009				
Profit. (%)	-12.8	-5.03	4.85	8.65	-6.39	71.8	2.34	1.07	2.03	0.2
INDEX	OMX Stockholm 30 Index									
Year	2007					2007				
Profit. (%)	-8.25	-6.94	2.98	2.12	-4.35	105.1	4.02	1.14	0.62	0.53
Year	2008					2008				
Profit. (%)	-14.2	-11.8	-12.5	-8.21	-5.81	84.61	1.18	0.64	0.94	0.31
Year	2009					2009				
Profit. (%)	-8.1	-3.53	4.38	6.68	-4.97	75.43	1.76	1.29	0.73	0.49

Source: Own calculations

As we can see, both robots show much better results, than the index strategies, during the crisis period 2008-2009.

In many ways, it becomes possible due to the fact that the robots can get positive returns as on the rising, as on the falling market, while the index strategy – is a strategy of growing market only.

3) At which "time dimension" (M5, M15, H1, H4, D1) can robot trading strategies show the biggest returns?

> ➢ Trading robot **Expert1** - based on the indicator EMAVFS (*trend following strategy*) – on all tested indexes - shows stable negative return at large time frame (D1) and at small time frames (M5, M15).
> But, at the same time, it shows steady positive returns at the medium time frames (H1, H4).
> This fact suggests that this trading strategy (*trend following strategy*) should be used for the intra-day trading, but not for high-frequency, or position trading.

> ➢ Trading robot **Expert2** - based on *statistical arbitrage* shows its' best results at the smallest time frame (M5), just like the theory "predicts" it. Moreover, in some market's phases, this strategy is capable to show an annual rate of return in the amount of 190.94%; 176%; 168.75% (See Figures in Appendix 4).

4) For which "market phases" (trend or flat) can robot trading strategies be used in the most optimal way?

> Trading robot **Expert1** shows the best results on trending market segments.
> As for the situation where the market is in a state of "flat", the returns of this robot are much less. This is also consistent with the theoretical basis of the strategy, since that strategy is based on exploitation of moving average, which reveals itself completely on the trend phases mostly.

5) Does "market efficiency" have the same value when we move from small to large "time dimension", and does it stable other considered period of time (2003 – 2012)?

> It is really indicative, how rapidly the returns of robot **Expert2** decrease, when we move to larger time frames! The difference in returns of the robot in different time frames within the same year can be 20-40 times!

> This fact can be regarded as confirmation of theory that the "market efficiency" increases with the transition to the larger time frames. Accordingly, the greater the time interval we consider, the more difficult to exploit the "inefficiencies" of markets!

> According to the results tables, returns of both robots have a tendency to decrease over time.

> Namely, the returns of algorithmic trading strategies, obtained in the beginning and in the end of the observing period, differ by several times!
> This fact also suggests that markets become more "efficient" over time, respectively, it becomes harder and harder to exploit the old algorithmic strategies without substantial revision and modification of them.

6 Conclusion

The main ambition of this research was the comparison of algorithmic trading and index investing' effectiveness in terms of returns and costs for strategy' implementation (like cost for developing information and trading infrastructure, brokerage cost, etc).

One of the main results of this study is the fact, that at the current phase of markets' development, it is theoretically possible for algorithmic trading (and especially high-frequency strategies) to exceed the returns of index strategy, but we should notice two very important factors:

1) Taking into account all of the costs of organization of high-frequency trading (brokerage and stock exchanges commissions, trade-related infrastructure maintenance, etc.), the difference in returns (with superiority of high-frequency strategy) will be much less (see more in section *4.3 Organization of trading infrastructure. Development of trading robots*).

2) Given the fact that "markets' efficiency" is growing every year (see more about it in the thesis), and the returns of high-frequency strategies tends to decrease with time (see more about it in the thesis), it is quite logical to assume that it will be necessary to invest more and more in trading infrastructure to "fix" the returns of high-frequency trading strategies on a higher level, than the results of index investing strategies.

It was shown, that market efficiency is increasing, if we move from small to large "time dimension" of observations and that market efficiency is increasing over the years.

According to theoretical observations, it was noted that high-frequency trading can provide market with liquidity, decrease spreads and helps align prices across markets, if it is implemented as market-making or arbitrage strategy. In terms of market volatility, it was not found any evidence for a detrimental impact of either algorithmic trading or high-frequency trading.

In future it would be interesting to test considered trading algorithms on a complete high-frequency scale, when the trading robots are located explicitly on stock exchange servers and it is possible to test them on real-time trading with every price-tick movements.

References

Aldridge, I. (2009). *High-Frequency Trading: A Practical Guide to Algorithmic Strategies and Trading Systems,* John Wiley & Sons

Andersen, T.G., T. Bollerslev, and F.X. Diebold (2007). Roughing It Up: Including Jump Components in the Measurement, Modeling and Forecasting of Return Volatility, *Review of Economics and Statistics,* 89, 701-720

Angel, J., Harris, L., Spratt, C. (2010). *Trading in the 21st Century,* available from http://www.sec.gov/comments/s7-02-10/s70210-54.pdf

Bank for International Settlements: High-frequency trading in the foreign exchange market, September 2011

Berstein, W. (2000). *The Intelligent Asset Allocator: How to Build Your Portfolio to Maximize Returns and Minimize Risk,* McGraw-Hill

Biais, B., Foucault, T., and Moinas S. (2010). Equilibrium Algorithmic Trading, Working Paper, Tolouse School of Economics

Brogaard, J. (2010). High Frequency Trading and Its Impact on Market Quality, Working paper, Northwestern University

Brownlees, Christian T ; Cipollini, Fabrizio ; Gallo, Giampiero M (2011). Intra-daily Volume Modeling and Prediction for Algorithmic Trading, *Journal of Financial Econometrics,* 9(3), pp. 489-518

Bulashev, S. (2010). *'The exponential moving average with a variable smoothing factor', Algorithmus,* no.3, pp. 37-41

Chaboud, A., Chiquoine, B., Hjalmarsson, E., Vega, C. (2009). Rise of the Machines: Algorithmic Trading in the Foreign Exchange Market, available from: http://ssrn.com/abstract=1501135

Chlistalla, M., High frequency trading – Better than its reputation, Research note, Deutsche Bank, February 2011

Colby, R.W. (2002). *The encyclopedia of trading market indicators,* 2nd ed., McGraw-Hill

Easley, Lopéz de Prado & O'Hara: *The microstructure of the"flash crash": Flow toxicity, liquidity crashes and the probability of informed trading,* November 2010

Edwards, R.D., Magee, J. (2007). *Technical Analysis of Stock Trends,* 9th ed., AMACOM

Fabocci, F (1995). *Investment management,* Prentice Hall

Finansinspektionen report, *Investigation into high frequency and algorithmic trading,* February 2012

Ferri, RA. (2002). *All about Index Funds: The Easy Way to Get Started,* McGraw-Hill Professional

Froot, K., Scharfstein, D. S., Stein, J.C. (1992). Herd on the Street: Informational Inefficiencies in a Market with Short-Term Speculation, *Journal of Finance,* 47, 1461-1484.

Galitz, L. (2002). *Financial Engineering – Tools and Techniques to Manage Financial Risk,* 3rd ed., Irwin Professional Publishing

Gibson, R.C. (2006). *Asset Allocation – Balancing Financial Risk,* 3rd ed., McGraw-Hill

Gomber, P. (2011). High Frequency Trading. Technical Report, Goethe Universität & Deutsche Börse;

Government Office for Science: The Future of Computer Trading in Financial Markets, 2011

Hasbrouck, J. (1996). Order characteristics and stock price evolution: An application to program trading, *Journal of Financial Economics,* 41, 129-149

Hasbrouck. J., & Saar., G., Low Latency Trading, New York University, 2010

Hendershott, T., and Riordan, R. (2009). Algorithmic Trading and Information, working paper, University of California at Berkeley

Hendershott,T., C. Jones and A. Menkveld (2011). Does Algorithmic Trading Improve Liquidity, *Journal of Finance,* 66, 1-33

Hoboken, N.J. (2009). Quantitative trading how to build your own algorithmic trading business, John Wiley & Sons

Jean-Pierre Zigrand, J-P., Cliff, D., Hendershott, T. (2010). Financial stability and computer based trading, available from:
http://www.bis.gov.uk/assets/foresight/docs/computer-trading/11-1276-the-future-of-computer-trading-in-financial-markets

Jorion, P., Goetzmann, W.N. (1999). Global stock markets in the twentieth century. *Journal of Finance.* 54(3), 953-980

Katz, J.O. (2000). *The encyclopedia of trading strategies,* McGraw-Hill

Kearns, M., Kulesza, A., Nevmyvaka, Y. (2010). Empirical Limitations on High Frequency Trading Profitability. *The Journal of Trading*, 5(4):50-62, Available from http://www.cis.upenn.edu/~mkearns/papers/hft_arxiv.pdf

Kendall, G., Chen, S.H., Binner, J.M. (2009). Applications of artificial intelligence in finance and economics, Bingley, Emerald Group Publishing Limited

Lati, R. (2009). *The Real Story of Trading Software Espionage*, Available from: <http://www.advancedtrading.com/algorithms/218401501>. [19 April 2012]

Linton, O., O'Hara, M. (2009). The impact of computer trading on liquidity, price efficiency/discovery and transaction costs, available from: http://www.bis.gov.uk/assets/foresight/docs/computer-trading/11-1276-the-future-of-computer-trading-in-financial-markets

Malkiel, BG. (1996). *A Random Walk Down Wall Street*, 4th ed., W. W. Norton

McDonald, R.D. (2005). *Derivatives Markets*, 2nd ed., McGraw-Hill

MetaQuotes Language 4, Language and Software Documentation, available from: http://docs.mql4.com/

Naiman, E. (2004). *Trader's small encyclopedia*, 7th ed., McGraw-Hill

O'Neal, E.S. (1997). How Many Mutual Funds Constitute a Diversified Mutual Fund Portfolio? *Financial Analysts Journal*, March/April, p. 37-46

Pardo, R. (1992). *Design, Testing and Optimization of Trading Systems*, Wiley, New York

Passive Index Investment Strategies are Superior (2007). Available from: <http://www.theskilledinvestor.com/wp/passive-index-investment-strategies-are-superior-57.htm>. [12 March 2007]

Perez, E. (2011). *The Speed Traders*, McGraw-Hill Publishers.

Pozen, R., Hamacher, T. (2011). *The Fund Industry: How Your Money is Managed*, John Wiley & Sons. pp. 11–14.

Pring, M. (2002). *Technical Analysis Explained: The Successful Investor's Guide to Spotting Investment Trends and Turning Points*, 4th ed., McGraw-Hill

Reuters (2011, July 7), *Ultra fast trading needs curbs-global regulators.*

Serebryannikov, D. (2011). Introduction to algorithmic trading, *Journal of Futures & Options,* no.4, pp.22-25

Sharpe, WF. (1991). The Arithmetic of Active Management, *The Financial Analysts' Journal,* no.3, pp.31-34

Sherry, C. (1992). *Mathematics of Technical Analysis,* Probus Professional Publisher

Simons, J., (2010, September 13), Flash Crash: High Frequency traders saved the Day, *Wall Street Journal,* p. B1

Smorodskay, P. (2010). MMVB vzylas za robotov\MICEX pays attention on robots, *Kommersant* 20 July, Available from: <http://www.kommersant.ru/doc/1455743>. [19 April 2012]

Tergesen, A., Young, L (2004). *Index Funds Aren't All Equal,* Bloomberg *Businessweek* 19 April, available from: <http://www.businessweek.com/magazine/content/04_16/b3879125_mz070.htm>. [19 April 2004]

Tolstousov, A. (2010). The splitting of the index core, *Algorithmus,* no.20, pp. 30-35